Gaslighting Recovery Workbook

How to Overcome Manipulation,
Narcissistic Abuse,
Codependency, and Heal
Yourself

Rita Hayes

Table of Contents

Introduction

Every single person will experience bad treatment from someone else many times in their life. Although this is an unfortunate "normal," there are boundaries for the kind of treatment that we should be willing to accept from others. From strangers, bad treatment is not really an issue, but it becomes an issue when we are in the line of fire from someone we are close to.

Before we can dive into gaslighting as a whole, it is important to understand what it is exactly, and how to spot it. Also, keep in mind that there are always two sides to a coin and we will explore both a little bit here.

In recent times, we have become more aware of abuse, thanks in no small part to social media platforms and groups of individuals who take the time to raise awareness. Their only intentions being to simply help victims turn their lives around and become survivors.

None of us are exempt from being abused or being abusive, we are all guilty in one way or another. The difference is whether we are receiving it or dishing it out. Abuse can push people to the point where somebody seriously gets hurt, to the point of almost no return to normality.

Abuse and mind games completely bend a person's perception of the world around them as well as their belief and trust in themselves. Enduring such abuse is brutal and cruel, and we should know better than to do it to others. Not all forms of manipulation are bad, but they can become quite harmful, even fatal in many cases. How we treat others is completely within our capabilities to understand and comprehend; how others treat us is not that simple. This does not mean, however, that we should allow it—and if we find ourselves in a position where we are being manipulated or gaslighted by someone else, especially those who claim to love and care about us, we need to take some steps to ensure our own sanity and a healthy mental and emotional state of being.

The aim of this book is to raise awareness when it comes to gaslighting abuse, manipulation, and narcissism. It is not to say we are in such a position, but because in this day and age, people tend to value things more than they do other people. The tendency to abuse others to reach personal goals is becoming less taboo and less concerning for the majority of the human population. We need to strive to be more open minded and learn to be more patient and caring towards each other, but mostly to ourselves.

Even though the road to a stress-free life is just about impossible, this does not mean that we simply should not or cannot be happy with our choices, and we certainly have the right to break ties with the people in our lives whose main goal is to bring us down in order to further their own agendas. The downside of relationships that fail, or even some that do not fail, is that someone always gets hurt. Even more so when there is disrespect and abuse involved.

Either one or both parties can be abusive in a relationship, and it can be any relationship, not just between lovers, but also parents, grandparents, coworkers, and friends. Just about any kind of relationship can have these nasty effects. What we need to do is to educate ourselves on how to manage such relationships.

This book will tell the story of a woman named Lisa, then briefly talk about her experiences from growing up, her failed marriage, and other relationships. This story was chosen to demonstrate how abuse can totally break a person down to nothing because of the various life events that shaped Lisa and altered her reality to such an extent that she felt she was not worthy of even having a life to live. What does it take for an abused person to draw the line, to say enough is enough and refuse any more unacceptable treatment from others? How far can and do things really go before we finally pull the plug?

Is everything that we experience and endure from others really worth the price we pay in the end, and to what end? Why do we feel that we cannot stick to boundaries we have set in order to protect ourselves from outside abuse? Who gave these people the right to treat us in such a way? Being emotionally abused certainly causes damage, and most of the time this gets passed on to our children. This fact needs to be acknowledged so we can break the cycle.

There are signs and symptoms that we can learn to understand and notice as soon as we realize that we have become unwilling victims in another person's selfish game to gain control and power. We need to take back our own power and refuse to let others trample us for their own selfish gain. It does not matter what they get out of it, what matters is how we take care of ourselves, and that we teach others how we deserve to be treated.

We must learn that we need to set boundaries and say no. Patience is a virtue that not many people have successfully mastered. This can be very important in the process of healing, recovering, and making very important decisions when we have had enough of the abuse and need to make some serious changes. Oftentimes, setting boundaries means having to break ties with people that we love and care about. How we handle ourselves in such desperate situations, and the fear of letting go of everything we know and love, is essential so that we can regain our identities and live life to the fullest again. We may not know the purpose of our time on earth, but we know that it is a very short time. So, it's up to us to make the best of it and give it our all, even in the face of ugly truths or the constant fear of failure that drives us in various directions on any given day.

While taking back our lives seems like a bit of a fairy tale, especially after enduring so much abuse and complete emotional breakdowns, it is definitely an achievable outcome. We need to remain motivated to become the best versions of ourselves even though it feels like we're fighting an ever-losing battle. All is not lost, we just have to be willing to take the risks and let go of what we know to be harmful for us.

There are many factors that play a role in an abusive relationship, and of course, the events taking place make us question ourselves and everyone and everything around us. There is also the question of why one person could act in such a way towards another person or how they can live with themselves knowing the damage they have caused.

Most abusers know full well what they are doing and what they are capable of. They can see the damage and the hurt, but when they are confronted, they laugh it off, feeding more into the idea of making their victim sound crazy. However, when the victim reaches out for help, the people they thought were friends simply do not feel the need to be supportive or even listen to their plight.

It is heartbreaking to behold such abuse, let alone live with it. From an outsider's point of view, it seems as though the abuser is the one being abused and that the other person is indeed probably crazy or going crazy. Very seldom would someone reach out to a victim because even these friends are victims of gaslighting abuse. The only difference with them is that the outside parties never experience the direct abuse as they are not the target of the abuser. They are simply coerced into believing whatever the abuser wants them to believe. As we can see here, the gaslighting abuser is certainly a master of their craft and there really is not much that can be done about it because we cannot change people. The only thing we can do is make our own changes and, hopefully, free ourselves from the circumstances that brought us into these positions in the first place.

As bystanders, the best we can do is to be open, available, and ready to listen should we be approached by someone who needs the help but may feel too ashamed to seek professional advice or disclose information to a stranger. It also helps when we are made aware of the signs of gaslighting abuse because, if so, we can spot the dangers in others and attempt to make them feel at ease when, or even encourage, they start seeking help. Nobody wants to think that people are capable of such evil, but it is a reality that we must all face. Instead of being judgmental, we need to open our hearts and minds to those in need, because we can all easily become victims, then we will need someone to go to in our time of need. There is no easy way to deal with abuse, whether we are the victim or we know the victim, but we simply cannot just walk away or turn the other cheek, no matter who the abuser may be.

Chapter 1:

Gaslighting Explained

Gaslighting in simple terms means that a person will target another, and over a period of time, start making them question their own truth or reality. This person is referred to as a "gaslighter," and a gaslighter will use various techniques to apply abuse into their daily lives. On the receiving end, the victim will end up feeling as if they are "going crazy." Gaslighting is indeed an extremely severe form of psychological abuse and may leave the victim feeling hopeless or helpless and, oftentimes, both.

Gaslighting abuse can happen in any kind of relationship; from our parents to our partners, and even in our workplace. It involves elements such as manipulation and narcissism which play on our emotional well-being and psychological health.

The worst part of being a victim in a gaslighting relationship is that we do not immediately realize what is happening, and more often than not, we learn the reality of the abuse much later or when we have reached the point that we are so lost that we cannot see a way out. When we are raised in such an environment, we become so bent that we become dependent on others and look for validation in all of the wrong places and from the wrong people. In turn, we will inflict this kind of abuse onto others, such as our own children, without even realizing it.

Even with only this little bit of information, it should be clear that gaslighting is very serious and its consequences are grave. Many of the phrases used by gaslighters are not always classified as abusive, but take into consideration the context of a conversation or situation. It is very easy to confuse actual gaslighting with a bit of innocent manipulation. Not all forms of manipulation and narcissism are negative projections towards another person. There is a very fine line, and of course, we need to be aware of this in order for us to appropriately deal with any harmful behavior towards us. In any relationship, we will experience some criticism, but we need to be aware of the difference between constructive criticism and blatant belittling.

It's important to note: The day that we wake up to abuse and decide to take action is when the abuser will come in full force. They will try every trick in the book to keep you from standing up and fending for yourself. It is simply unacceptable to them that you would stand up for yourself, and they cannot deal with it. They will usually leave first as a last show of power over us to make it clear how weak we are and how they will always win. The secret is to not let them see you in a weakened state or give them the satisfaction of winning their game. Lisa's husband was furious when she decided enough was enough and made a plan to get away from him. He continued to bring her down and laughed at every attempt she made to get some form of justice for her situation. She filed for divorce, but he refused to see it through at first because, as another attempt to prove his power over her, she had to fight for her freedom. She expected him to fight for custody of their children but he did not, and this completely baffled Lisa. She believed that he would at least try, and when he did not, it was obvious that he was throwing her another curveball. One last shot at attacking her and her attempts to get better.

Signs of Gaslighting

While there are many signs of gaslighting, there are only a handful that we might experience on a daily basis, which means we do not think much about it but rather accept it as normal. These signs include:

- Continuous lying: The gaslighter will always lie. What makes it worse is how easy it is for them to tell the lies to your face without even blinking. This is one of the most brutal ways in which a gaslighter can manipulate and overpower their victim in an instant.

- Words versus actions: Gaslighters will very often contradict themselves. They talk the talk, but simply cannot walk the walk. Their words differ from their actions as daytime differs from the nighttime.

- You change according to their wishes: Over time, while you slowly start to question who you are, you become more and more the person they want you to be. You're no longer comfortable to be "you."

- They are emotionally breaking you down: Your opinions do not seem to matter, and if they do, you will come to find that, sooner or later, those opinions will be used against you in order for the abuser to control you even more.

- You begin to feel as if you are going crazy: It is right here where you start to doubt yourself and your reality, making it possible for the abuser to bend your reality.

- They twist or bend your reality: At this stage of the abuse, you are completely vulnerable to their whims and believe what they tell you to be true, unable to tell the difference between what is real and what is not. In other words, you have been brainwashed.

- They will find issues with everything: They will question everything you say, withhold information to confuse you, and even bad-mouth you to others to make it seem like you are going crazy or unstable.

Common Words or Phrases Used by Gaslighters

Notice in the following phrases how the target is always in the wrong:

- "You are overreacting! Calm down."

- "What you say does not make sense."

- "I cannot remember this."

- "You are so sensitive."

- "You are imagining things."

Although there are many more examples, the ones mentioned are used most often, and it seems like these words hold the most power when it comes to breaking you down emotionally and mentally.

Another notable aspect of gaslighters is the fact that they are often pathological liars. Once you suspect that you are dealing with a gaslighter, it is necessary to verify much of the information that they share. It is also very important not to get involved in any arguments whatsoever. It may sound quite a cliche, but it is true when it is said that whatever the case, in an argument they will beat you with experience. They become so good at telling lies that they probably believe them and will go out of their way to convince you of the same.

You will find yourself apologizing for things you do not even know that you did. Once you are at this stage, you have been changed already. It is very sad to think of how easy it is to fall victim to such abuse. It starts out so subtle that you do not realize that the situation or relationship is slowly breaking you down. Given a few months, you find yourself questioning everything, and it is a downward spiral from there if you do not notice and address the change.

Discovering that not only have you been devalued but that you were never an actual object of affection but rather a target for being overpowered for someone else's selfish benefit is a horrible thought. However, most people go through relationships and their entire lives without realizing the damage that is being done or has been done.

The secret is to be aware of our circumstances and take note of how we are spoken to in conjunction with the current topic or context of the topic. If we are being disrespected, we should definitely ask ourselves why and if it is worth saying something about it or better to just leave it alone. For the most part, we do not ask these questions because we often just accept that the person we are communicating with just acts this way. This approach is normal, but we need to look into how we are treated a little more when it comes to someone in our close vicinity that we deal with every day.

Chapter 2:

Manipulation

Manipulation is the art of changing the views or perceptions of another individual or group of individuals. Although it is not always an act of evil, it is a tactic commonly used by people to control others for their own benefit and it often leads to some damaging effects. This form of abuse is also often used by gaslighters in an attempt to gain control over their victims. Little by little, the manipulator will start expressing negativity about another person until said person starts to buy into the negative viewpoint. From there, it becomes a complete downward spiral into absolute dependence of the victim on the manipulator. Remember that this process does not always occur overnight. In many cases, it can take a few months or even years, depending on the end goal of the abuser, as well as the vulnerability of the victim.

Empaths are especially easy targets for gaslight abusers due to the fact that they generally do not differentiate themselves from their abuser, and they do not always know how to say "no." Empaths are individuals who have trouble setting boundaries for themselves, and thus, become such easy targets for manipulation and abuse.

However unfortunate it is, manipulation can occur anywhere, at any time. Another great example of manipulation and abuse is that of cult leaders, such as Jim Jones and Charles Manson. These two men succeeded in making other people hang onto every word they uttered and commit some heinous crimes. Jim Jones and his cohorts managed to convince hundreds of people (all his followers of the People's Temple, which he founded), including children, to commit "revolutionary suicide." Charles Manson also had quite the manipulative skill set. He easily convinced a small group of young people to commit the murder of Sharon Tate and her friends. These two events alone prove how powerful gaslighting really is, and how easy anyone can fall victim to such abuse. This type of manipulation is an extreme form of narcissism, but it is important to remember that not all forms of manipulation lead to narcissism.

Manipulation happens all around us, and it is quite harsh when it is our parents who use this tactic to control us.

Parents Who Use Manipulation to Control Their Children

The following story is a very good example of parental manipulation and its long-term effects.

Lisa grew up with her mother, stepfather, and half-sister. Her parents divorced when she was still a baby and soon after, both parents remarried. Lisa was always permitted visitation with her father, but only did so when she was a little older, which means the only family she knew until then were those she lived with. Lisa simply cannot remember a truly happy time during her childhood. Keep in mind here that as a young child, even a teenager, she believed her life at home was normal and that everybody experienced the same type of lifestyle. When I asked Lisa about her relationship with her mother, she said that they did not really have a good relationship. Perhaps when she was younger, she was made to believe it was a good relationship, but while growing up and becoming her own person and having more and more contact with the outside world, she realized just how warped her reality really was.

She began giving examples of her life by saying her mother was not a very faithful woman. Her first memory of unfaithfulness from her mother's side happened long before she knew or understood the sanctity of marriage and relationships. Her mother once took her along to meet up with a man she had never met before. The two adults were just talking, and only much later did it surface that her mother had an affair with this man. In another instance, her mother and stepfather had an argument and her mother went out for the evening, taking her along. What happened next shocked Lisa very much. They ended up visiting a friend of her mother and his friend. Later in the evening, when the party died down, her mother decided it would be better to sleep over instead of driving home. The two men shared a room in a house they were renting, and while her mother got into bed with her friend, Lisa had to share a single bed with the man's friend. Her mother had sex with this man she was now sharing the bed with, all in the same room, and at the same time this was happening, the other man made advances toward Lisa. She did not say much more about the event itself, but it was clear that the situation affected Lisa in a very negative manner.

When looking at this situation, one can only imagine what must have been going through Lisa's mind at the time. This is only the beginning of all the wrongs Lisa had to face during her young life, but this alone is enough to start painting a picture of what her childhood was like. Later on, Lisa talked about the physical abuse and mental abuse that led to a complete breakdown of her character. The sad part is that Lisa did not even realize that she was being pushed to a break down. Can you imagine always being told that you ruined your mother's life, or that you are a constant disappointment? One account Lisa recalls is when she was about nine- or ten-years-old and always looked forward to taking part in school sports. On one such occasion, Lisa chose short distance running. On the day of the race, she finished last, and it was made clear to her that her mother was embarrassed. Needless to say, Lisa slowly developed a negative complex when it came to sports, but this was not the only element of life that Lisa had issues with. It was her looks, her weight, her choices, her actions, and even her feelings that came under scrutiny from her mother.

Often times when people have an issue with a certain aspect of their bodies, it can be fixed. For example, if you are not fit enough but wish to be, you can go to the gym or find another means to reach this goal. Other times, the body issues are embedded much deeper to the point where no matter how much we do and how good we look, we are never happy and will find strange ways to achieve certain desired aspects of our bodies, such as lip injections to create a fuller appearance. Both men and women have these issues, and they can start at a young age.

We have all heard of "grooming," and most of the time, it is never meant in a good way. There are stories of adult women speaking out about being groomed and the abuse they suffer under their superiors, especially in the entertainment industry. Grooming like this happens privately as well, and is not limited to the rich and famous. It also does not always happen the way we see it on television. There are various ways that people find to groom their victims, mostly from a very young age. The tendency to groom someone could also be a sign of narcissism from the side of the abuser. Referring back to Lisa's story, she mentioned that her mother made it very clear to her husband that he was not Lisa's father and that any discipline would be handled by her. In turn, this created a rift between Lisa and her stepfather, which carries on to this day. It is very heartbreaking to think about this because Lisa had basically been raised by this man since she was practically still in diapers. Sadly, Lisa's mother had already passed away by the time she was ready to confront some of the abuse she had endured, therefore, she will never really receive the answers she so desperately needs.

Although Lisa's story has many more details, the ones mentioned are more than enough to demonstrate how a parent can manipulate their children. Also, how putting them in the middle of adult issues can break a young person even before they have discovered themselves. This is just one of so many examples of how young adults fall into the wrong social circles, as well as how the cycle of abuse continues when they choose their life partner. Either the victim will try and find someone they can find familiarity with in comparison to their upbringing, or they become manipulators and gaslighting abusers themselves. The line here is indeed very thin, as the victim often does both. It is understandable why a victim may want to seize control over their own lives and their very selves. It's also easy to see how this desire pushes them to find someone they can in turn push around. It is a cold truth, and the vicious cycle needs to end somehow.

Dealing With Manipulation

There are a few things to remember when dealing with manipulative people, especially parents. For starters, one needs to understand where this type of behavior comes from. Keep in mind that most of the time, parents do not even realize the kind of damage they have enforced on their child(ren).

In terms of a manipulating mother, for example, there are some signs to take note of:

- Verbal abuse.

- Guilt-tripping you when you attempt to set boundaries.

- You are called "rude" when you try to stand up for yourself.

- She never apologizes for her behavior.

- Your mother prefers you to be dependent on her, and ensures it.

- She places her needs above anyone else's, even you.

- She will play favorites with the children as it suits her.

- You are forced to continuously do things for her, whether you agree with it or not.

- Nothing you do is ever good enough, no matter how hard you try to make her happy.

- She may use the silent treatment to get her disapproval across. This is another form of manipulation used on you to break you down even more.

- She is a pathological liar and has the ability to make people believe she is a completely different person.

- When you do not behave according to her desires, she may threaten you or belittle you.

- She uses gaslighting ways to manipulate you, twisting things to the point that you question your own truths and memory of events

- She constantly uses guilt to make you please her.

- Because manipulators are not generally happy, she will create drama and watch it unfold, especially during holidays or at special gatherings.

- She is constantly trying to steer you in the direction of living your life in ways that she had always wanted to live.

- No matter how happy you are or whatever good happens to you, she will never be happy for you. It will almost seem as if she is harboring slight jealousy or envy towards you.

Most of the points above can apply to all manipulative relationships, not just from mothers, or parents, or even grandparents, but also to people we believe are good friends or our partners. The reason that this is used as an example of parental manipulation is to demonstrate how deep such abuse can go, and how it can even come from those who we love and look up to the most. You will find that in the end, we will always be looking for approval from this person, but in the long run, we realize that we will never receive it.

Even though these facts are disheartening, we must accept that we cannot change another person. All that we can do is change how we choose to respond to them, and how we deal with it further on in our lives (especially if we do not have any other choice, such as walking away from a relationship).

Choose rather to limit contact with this person, and continue to set boundaries, even if it upsets the other person. We need to show the abusive person that we will no longer stand for this behavior, then express our desire to be treated better and with more respect, to be acknowledged as a human being, and to accept that what they are doing is not okay. It is also helpful to seek some counseling to obtain the tools to deal with the person on an ongoing basis, and to prevent you from becoming discouraged if it's not accepted or changed as quickly as you'd like.

What often happens in abusive relationships is that when we feel trapped, we start looking for coping mechanisms, and more often than not, we find ourselves in the midst of everything that is unhealthy.

Chapter 3:

Narcissistic Abuse

Narcissism is another form of manipulation; however, this type of abuse is much more severe due to the fact that narcissism can have fatal consequences. A narcissistic person will consciously be on the attack psychologically and will use whichever manipulative means necessary to reach their goals. Narcissists are usually people with extreme admiration for, or interest in, themselves. This fact alone is not necessarily an issue, but it does differ from person-to-person, and there is a type of narcissism connected to "psychopath." Most cases of narcissism begin during childhood.

Many people find themselves in narcissistic relationships of some kind. One of the worst, however, is when it is part of intimate relationships and marriages. Recalling Lisa's story, we will look at how she explained her marriage. She married a man who had been a good friend for a few years, and who she thought would be the perfect man to build a family with. It did not take very long for her to realize that her reality was not what she was hoping for or expecting.

She was pregnant with their first child when her husband decided that she was not giving him enough attention and went out to look for it elsewhere. This would happen often, but he would deny it even though she would have some type of evidence. This situation is quite difficult to deal with especially given the fact that Lisa was pregnant at the time. Another important point to mention is due of her history with her mother, she was made to believe that because she had chosen this partner, she had to accept whatever the relationship would come with. Thus, complaining about it would be a sign of weakness or betrayal to her husband. This is a terrible thought, indeed, but this is how broken Lisa already was. Her self-esteem was low enough for her to stay loyal, she felt that now that they are starting a family; it would be for the best to stick it out. Not long into the relationship her husband was cheating, looking for other women's attention, but still expected Lisa to be home raising the kids. On top of all that, she still had to maintain a full-time job.

To give an idea of what her relationship with her husband was like, here are some incidents to map out a few of the events that took place:

- He would openly be unfaithful to Lisa while she was at work or at home with the children.

- When she would find out or suspect this type of behavior, he would either deny it or say things like "if you cannot prove it, then it did not happen."

- On one occasion, he left his phone unlocked knowing she suspected him of having an affair, and she would use the opportunity to gain some kind of evidence.

- When she finally had proof, he would play it down and blame her for the affair, then would ask for a divorce. He expected her to accept his extra-marital relationships and either make things work for everybody or just leave, knowing she had nowhere to go and two children to take care of.

- When she then opted to leave the marriage and find a way to survive, he would often hold against her the fact she had to leave her children behind for a short time.

- He continued to break her down and planned to convince a judge that she abandoned the children so he could gain full custody of them.

- When he realized that his affair was not working out, he used her vulnerability and fear of losing her children to get her back with him.

- From there on, things did get really sticky, but in the process, she had made some friends and built a metaphorical bridge for her to get away from him. So, this time, she was taking her children with her.

Lisa learned some lessons here, but the problem was that Lisa was far from being fully equipped to deal with the aftermath. The final straw that caused her to leave him was when she was informed by a previous boss that her husband was up to his old tricks again. She contacted his mother and explained the situation. His mother understood very well, but also told Lisa that if she forgives him once more and stays with him, then she cannot use this against him again. His mom said she would need to forgive and forget and continue to work at making the marriage work. Lisa had to take a few days to think the situation over and make some very difficult decisions. It is not fair for anybody to have to live this way and she was fearful that if she stayed, her children would become the kind of people she was now trying to get away from. She felt it best to remove them completely and decided that it was time to move on. She filed for divorce and gained custody of the children without a fight from her husband.

What is also important to mention here is when the last argument happened, he physically attacked her and nearly killed her. He clearly did not appreciate the fact that Lisa was now, suddenly, standing up for herself and refusing to entertain his selfishness any longer.

The day she made the decision, she felt a breath of freedom, and in her mind, it was the beginning of a new life, no matter how hard the road ahead may seem. All she knew at that point in time was that she no longer needed to be stuck in such a brutal situation. This relationship had stemmed from the influence of the relationship she had with her mother. She realized, as well, that she was looking for attention and approval from the wrong person. Although Lisa and her husband used to be great friends before they entered into a relationship, nothing could prepare her for what was to unfold during her marriage. She felt that through the marriage she was finally getting away from abuse and would have the opportunity to build a good life outside the clutches of her mother, and at the same time maintain a good relationship with her mother, especially after her children were born. Even with a strained relationship between her and her mother, Lisa was still able to talk to her mother and get some kind of support. A shocking fact that she discovered after the passing of her mother, was the fact that her relationship would escalate into something horrific with her husband. That is when his true colors began to show and he became openly deceitful and completely manipulative. A situation like this causes a lot of conflict within oneself because not only do these people break you down and make you into someone you are not, but you end up in the middle of nowhere with no real emotional support. Oftentimes in this situation, you do not know which way to go. So, all she knew is that she had to rebuild her life in the best way possible, even more so because she had something to prove to her children.

Signs of a Narcissistic Relationship

Being in a narcissistic relationship is one of the harshest truths we may have to face at some point or another in our lives. Most of us are often narcissistic, while others are on the receiving end. It is also important to note that we all have narcissistic tendencies, but most of us do not use them to harm others.

- A narcissistic person basically worships themselves and will devalue you and everything you believe or stand for.

- At first, they will make you feel like the most special person in the world, but once you believe it, the slow abuse begins.

- They will try to isolate you from friends and family as much as possible but not as obvious in the beginning.

- What catches your attention about them is a certain charm. They quickly learn how to get your attention and keep it; in other words, you get completely sucked into their game and become a "willing" victim.

- It often appears as though they have multiple personalities. We are who we are, our personalities remain consistent, and we portray this person to people we trust. With narcissists, it is a bit different. They will portray different personalities to different people, slip up sometimes, and may even get confused about who they are with you.

- At the start of the relationship, they will regard your feelings and show empathy, however, this does not last very long. Soon they come to belittle you and your feelings and disregard your thoughts or opinions. They lose patience with you. They lose interest in your interests, and everything becomes about them and them alone.

- They expect you to believe that the life you are living is just the way things are; they won't support any positive changes even if it benefits you both. They may make you feel like you cannot do anything better than them.

- They have no problem displaying any form of jealousy towards you. They are all about status and power, so once you show that you have things under control or are doing better than they are, they will try to make you feel like you are not deserving of your rewards.

- A very prominent feature of a narcissist is that they love to play the victim. They will exclusively look for, or create, trouble and play on your triggers, but when you have had enough and retaliate, they will turn the situation around to make it seem as though everything is your fault.

- They refuse to take any kind of responsibility for their actions, will badmouth you to others, and continuously play the victim card, making you out to be the monster to garner sympathy from everyone around them. If you try to get out of such a relationship with them, they will come after you even stronger. They refuse to lose you before they are through with you, and it puts a serious dent in their ego if they cannot maintain you as a victim until they find another victim

How to Deal With a Narcissistic Relationship

When you are in a relationship with a narcissist, you need to make some harsh decisions. You can stay in the relationship or you can walk away from it. It can never be both. If you decide to stay, you need to be vigilant to the same degree as you would if you were in a relationship with a manipulator. You must set boundaries, learn to say no, and not accept any abusive behavior towards you. Remember that relationships like this are dangerous and will destroy a person completely if not kept in check.

Another danger from such a relationship is that when you do decide to leave it behind, you may fall into another relationship of the same caliber. It is of utmost importance to take time off from any new relationship to find yourself again, even if it takes a very long time. Cutting the ties between the past and the present is very challenging; and it will test you on a daily basis, but remember that a journey of healing is about you and your future. It is very easy to give in to old habits or any kind of familiarity, so creating a safe haven for yourself should constantly be one of your top priorities.

Lisa made the mistake of getting into another relationship too soon after she broke free from her abusive husband. She did not allow herself time to heal from the ordeal or to find her voice again. She felt that she was ready to move on, but she was almost immediately infatuated with the new interest that she received from someone else. This is where that fine line of comfort versus challenge comes in. Instead of taking the time to build her life and improve, she devoted more time to trying to build this new relationship. One cannot blame Lisa; she has children and one of her goals and dreams was to build a stable home with loving parents for her children. Her mother was no longer there and everyone else had their own lives to live. She also did not want to be alone. Through her choices, we can see how the abuse had made her codependent. She needed to be in a relationship to be happy and to feel loved and like she belonged.

In an abusive relationship, the victims can take so much away from themselves without really coming to terms with any of it. Past experience is important so that we can learn to cope and handle future situations much better. We must always try to locate the positive things in past experiences, not only what we have learned but what we can teach others. As much as we try to protect our children from abuse, it would be impossible for them to avoid it for them their entire lives. The best thing that we can do is to make them aware of the dangers, without becoming abusive towards them as well. We need to make a habit of practicing the good on a daily basis because we quickly forget our goals in this regard, just like Lisa did for a moment. She forgot about her own end goal and once again got sucked into another charming relationship. Although this relationship was not with a narcissistic person, it was a case of tables turning and Lisa becoming abusive towards her new partner as a way to regain control of her own life. She didn't allow time to establish a form of authority that she was never allowed to have during her life up until this very point.

Needless to say, this relationship did not work out well for Lisa either. The ending of this relationship did more damage to her direct daily life than any of the other relationships could. Here is why:

- Her codependence made her accept the first bit of affection she received from another person.

- She was so desperate to break away from her past that she felt starting a new life with someone new would solve all her problems.

- She did not spend enough time on her own to give herself the much-deserved time to heal fully, reassess her life, and decide which road to take.

- It would have benefitted her more had she spent more time with her children, not to say that she did not, but her time was divided between them, her job, and finding space for a new person in her life.

- She didn't think about how the crumbling of her marriage might have affected her children.

- Lisa spent more time caring about what others thought of her and her choices than she spent time fixing the things she was not happy with.

- When the last relationship ended, she lost more than ever; things were so bad that she had to sell everything she ever worked for to survive and had to send her children to their father because, financially, she could not take care of them.

- After all was said and done, she was unable to trust anybody, even her closest friends who would never even think of causing her any harm.

Lisa's story is quite horrific, and of course, a very good example of how twisted and horrifying it is to grow up with abuse the way she has. It was only after the last relationship failed, that she finally realized the importance of learning from her past and that it was time to break the abusive cycle.

For a long period of time, she doubted herself and her choices. The buildup to the events that lead to her failures, her blaming herself, and taking her issues out on those she loved all played a part in her own destruction. Things went very sour, very fast after the last breakup, and she could not cope any more than she could function like a normal person. Everything was torn away from her. Lisa attempted suicide because of her hopelessness. She fully believed at this stage that she was a complete waste of space and that everyone would be better off if she was no longer around.

In her situation, we cannot judge as we cannot even begin to understand her journey, but we can learn some very important lessons here. It is very clear that she never learned, or was never taught, how to deal with narcissistic abuse and even accepted it as a normal way of life. She noted that she had also suffered from mild depression (probably due to her childhood drama and trauma) and, perhaps, hoped that acceptance from others might make her feel better about herself. When she figured out that others would not give her the validation she needed, she realized that she needed to get to know herself again, to trust her own instincts, and love herself once more. It is never too late.

Remember that the narcissist wants you to think that you are going crazy, and if you feel that this is the case, you would want to be able to put the puzzle pieces together to see the full picture much better. Staying on top of things can be difficult, but once again, learn to trust your instincts and listen to that little voice in your head. Our intuition is a great skill that we often overlook because we put more trust in the words of another person than we do in ourselves, and this is one of the things a narcissist knows very well. Once they realize that there is a vulnerable spot, they will latch onto that. You then will not see them coming or realize that they have already trapped you in their web of deceit and lies. As a victim, we buy into it completely because of that thick layer of charm they use to win us over.

Even though we might successfully break free from bad relationships, and start working on ourselves to regain some parts of us that were lost, there will always be remaining issues that will constantly need our attention. The next step is one of the hardest to overcome: codependency.

Chapter 4:

Codependency

The term "codependency" normally refers to an unhealthy relationship with someone who suffers from addiction. When we think of addiction, the first thought that comes to mind is drug or perhaps alcohol addiction. Although codependency is not classified as a type of personality disorder, it does overlap with borderline personality disorder (BPD) and dependent personality disorder (DPD), and even post-traumatic stress disorder (PTSD). If the mentioned terms refer to psychological disorders, the question is then what exactly do codependency, gaslighting, and narcissism possibly have in common? Well, quite a lot. Many of the symptoms of codependency may stem from long periods of mental abuse. Think about an empath for a moment. An empath shares many similarities with someone who suffers from codependency (take note there is a slight difference between a codependent and DPD; codependency refers to someone being dependent on one specific person, while DPD refers to someone who is codependent on anyone in general).

Symptoms of codependency include:

- Anxiety: Constantly feeling anxious is a common feeling experienced in a codependent relationship. We will find that the feeling of anxiety forms part of every other symptom we may be experiencing in a codependent relationship.

- Stress: This should be self-explanatory. Stress is part of life as much as our daily routine, however, when we open our eyes in the morning and the first thing we do is begin stressing over things that have not even happened yet, it becomes an issue. It is here where we start our negative thinking and start expecting everything to go wrong all the time. We are always anticipating bad things to happen, even if we have no reason to.

- Low self-esteem: Our self-esteem is one of our most valued possessions, and most of us struggle with it from time to time. It becomes unhealthy when our self-esteem is being challenged on a daily basis because in most abusive situations it is so easy to be broken down by the other person.

- Having trouble expressing emotions: Because of low self-esteem, in this case, we tend to want to control how others feel; in other words, we want everyone around us to be okay. We cannot express ourselves and oftentimes, when we have the need to speak up, it is almost as if we are projecting. In the long run, what would then happen is that those emotions we keep bottled up, then find their way to the surface. This can only lead to conflict, which in turn causes us to be very misunderstood. This too becomes an endless cycle if we are not aware of where the conflict is stemming from.

- Signs of narcissism: This point directly connects to the aforementioned. Our need to control others and their feelings is a sign of narcissism, and probably a symptom we cannot avoid in the midst of all the chaos already playing out in our minds and emotional state. It is important to take into consideration that codependency and narcissism can live under the same umbrella. The fine line between being an abuse victim and becoming an abuser is very real here, and differentiating between the two may be impossible.

- Familial dysfunction: This symptom is very common in homes where one or other addiction is involved, however, it is not limited to these homes. There might instead be plenty of anger issues for example. The point is that the dysfunctional family member will be the one who basically refrains from interacting on a normal basis with family members and chooses to rather keep to themselves. This may sound much like an introvert, but the difference here is that it is the addiction that separates family members and not just a perfectly normal personality trait. It is almost as though this person is hiding something all the time.

- Confusing love with pity: In many relationships, especially in the aftermath of one that has ended, we discover that what we thought was love that we were giving, even if we gave our all, was, in reality, only pity. It is said that it takes much time and work to overcome a dissolved relationship, but many times we find ourselves "over" the relationship quite quickly. This could be a sign that we never truly loved the other person, but rather displayed pity.

- Having little to no boundaries: Even when we have strong boundaries in life in general, when we fall into an abusive relationship, we put so much trust in the other person that we diminish our boundaries in order to make the other person happy. Once again, we become dependent on their approval in the unhealthiest of ways.

- Obsessing over mistakes: These are the things we allow to keep us awake at night, depriving ourselves of some much-needed beauty sleep. There is nothing wrong with overthinking any situation as it happens to most of us, but it becomes problematic when it is the only thing we can focus on.

- Caring too much about what others think of you and your actions: Something like this can definitely hold us back in life. This is a problem if we allow too much room for others' opinions in our daily lives. This is also one of the hardest issues to overcome as it is very much part of our daily lives and our way of thinking or feeling.

- Experiencing intimacy issues: This is quite the conundrum. We all long for personal relationships and intimacy, but because we are filled with so much doubt towards ourselves already, it makes it that much harder to open up on such a personal level, and letting go of all the stress from our lives even for short periods of time in order to enjoy these moments becomes nearly impossible, making this part of our relationships excruciatingly painful or stressful.

- Having a hard time saying no: We all experience moments where we find it hard to say no to someone to avoid some conflict, but it does not become an issue. In this case, however, we cannot say no because it will hinder our attempts to receive the approval we so desperately need from the other person.

- Wanting to be liked by everyone: Everyone wants to be liked by others, even when we do not realize it. In a case of a codependent relationship, we seek the constant approval of one person. This trait connects to being in a narcissistic/manipulative relationship because the other person has managed to break us down to the point where we do not feel of value unless they approve of everything we do.

- The need to always be in a relationship: This is one of the "uglier" signs of codependency. We are in a position where we feel lost when we are alone, or not in an actual relationship. Being in a close relationship with someone else is our way of feeling that we have a place in the world, like we belong. We think being in a relationship will fulfill our constant need to feel loved (however warped this may be), and our need to feel like we are cared for by someone else, instead of being happy on our own or loving ourselves enough to value our own time and our relationship with ourselves.

- Problems with communicating honestly: We are often confronted with wanting to make others happy above all else, so we will refrain from expressing our true thoughts and feelings because the other person may not agree, or we may take away from their happiness and satisfaction.

- Reacting emotionally most of the time: This is due to the fact that we have trouble communicating honestly and truthfully toward the other person. Again, we put our own needs and feelings at the back of the pack so that we can ensure the happiness of the other person.

- Feeling the need to have some control over others or the need to always take care of other people: In other words, we feel the need to fix others. Perhaps we feel lost, so in order to take control we want to fix other people.

- Displaying or expressing fear of abandonment or rejection: Most of us are not too worried about being rejected as it is part of life. We have accepted the fact that we will not be liked or adored by everyone we ever meet but, in some cases, we do suffer from the fear of rejection. We want to be liked because we do not like or value ourselves for the most part of our lives. We need acceptance, and being liked and accepted even by complete strangers becomes a priority. Our fear of rejection or abandonment may make us seem desperate, but our intentions are pure as far as we believe. We just want to be loved and accepted.

- Detachment: This connects to a previous point, but in this case, we are referring to a person being detached from the rest of the world, not just from family members. The person may have the desire to be social and make friends, but will not put in the effort because there is no real emotional connection found here, even though the need is there.

- Silence: Being silent is another symptom of codependency. There is a difference between being a quiet person and being silent. A quiet person can be perfectly happy in their own company with no underlying issues at all, while a silent person does not express themselves out of fear of judgment or rejection.

- Inability to trust others: A codependent person will not easily trust another person. This could be because of childhood trauma and/or their ongoing self-esteem issues. A codependent person will find that they can hardly trust themselves, so trusting another person entirely is almost impossible.

- Identity: Codependents do not usually have an identity of their own. They do not take the time to get to know themselves and thrive like any other person. Instead, they would subconsciously pay attention to others' personalities and "inherit" some of their traits and apply it to their own lives.

- They do not often take responsibility for their actions. For the most part, it is because they do not realize the seriousness of some conflict they might have stirred up, and even if they do, it is often noted that the codependent person does not understand that they did anything wrong or hurt someone else. Keep in mind here the point of detachment. This is not the same as a blatant narcissist, but rather a sign of narcissism which plays a large role in self-esteem and control issues.

- Making decisions is a chore: For codependents, it is very difficult to make decisions on their own. They often need assistance or approval from the person they are dependent on to steer their thoughts and feelings about a situation. This is not a case of being interested in a mere opinion or another point of view, but an absolute inability to make a simple decision regarding basic things. This also connects to how we care too much about what others may think.

- Taking too much responsibility: Here we are referring to the codependent taking on another person's responsibilities or overdoing tasks. This is mostly to avoid any conflicts at times; other times it is simply to find recognition. It is almost as if the codependent is constantly seeking praise to feel better about themselves.

The signs and symptoms above make quite a long list, and some do point to other forms of mental health issues, hence the fact that some disorders here overlap quite a bit. It would be better to seek a professional opinion instead of diagnosing oneself, however, recognizing these signs is a very good starting point on the road to recovery.

Keep in mind that everyone who experiences these symptoms has different backgrounds with different stories and circumstances, and this is why it is important to take the time to get to know yourself a little bit. Digging a little deeper, use these symptoms to try to figure out where these issues stem from and also, to identify those who were abusive to you in the past.

Being codependent in an abusive relationship or even in the aftermath does not make you a bad or a weak person. It only goes to show how you have been affected and how much of yourself you have given in the relationship already. Always remember that when we choose (or not choose) to love someone we make the decision to give up who we are to that person and they can basically do with it as they wish. Just by being in a relationship we've already given so much power to the other person. We share our lives, our time, our space, our secrets, everything. We basically hand power to the abuser on a silver platter.

In a manner, we are all dependent on each other. It becomes a bit of an issue when we become too dependent and an abuser absolutely loves this advantage. It gives them the opportunity to exploit their victim who will in turn depend on the abuser more and more. Even in the event of breaking up the relationship, the victim will carry this feeling that they constantly need someone with them through, or until they realize it is just a symptom of the abuse they experienced. Getting out of those abusive clutches can be quite terrifying because suddenly you have to be alone, and you do not even know how to be by yourself. Building new friendships to fill the void also does not seem to work because there is a specific level of intimacy required that cannot be found between mere friends. It is important here to figure out who you are without the other person and their influence. What is it about them that you need so much, and why? We all hunger for unconditional love in our relationships, but it is not always the case that we receive it. In many relationships, we either love more than the other person does or even less than they do and finding that balance can be quite tricky. If you feel like you are potentially codependent but do not want to walk away from the relationship, you may want to take a break to figure things out for yourself. Remember that all of this is a part of a healing process. The fact is that nobody can really tell you what to do because as humans we are stubborn when it comes to matters of the heart and this is why we have such a hard time making decisions when it comes to love and relationships. We may follow advice or open our minds to our friends observing our behavior around certain people and perhaps give it some thought, but the fact is that we seldom take the advice to heart until it is probably too late. Those same friends are the ones who will gladly help us pick up the pieces, even after we could not be bothered with considering that their warnings may have been correct.

Also, in a codependent relationship, we become used to the other person steering the relationship most of the time. This also relates to the codependent person becoming fearful within the relationship; such as constant anxiety that you keep doing things the wrong way or that you do not make your partner happy enough. Chances are that you would have had a dependency issue before getting into this relationship, and the fact your partner is abusive only worsens all those fears of rejection or criticism.

The best solution is to find outside help for this. As bad as abuse in itself is, being dependent on an abuser makes everything much worse and can significantly slow down the healing process. Learning to not be dependent is one of the hardest things to do in life and many people never get past it, even if they do overcome most of the other elements of abuse that they have suffered along the way.

The reason for this is that even if you win back all your confidence and self-esteem, the need to be with someone never really goes away. It is much like having to accept the demise of a loved one. You learn to live with it, but you may never feel like you are getting used to it or learn to enjoy your own company and appreciate your precious time with yourself. Codependency is a sign of insecurity. It is also connected with our need to constantly be validated. We struggle to find a healthy balance, in this regard, and will probably share our time and energy with anyone showing us some type of attention or affection. Whether it is in physical form or not, we always need to get attention from someone.

Codependency reflects Lisa's story because at the first sign of affection she jumped straight into her next relationship without even thinking. At the time this happened, Lisa did not even fully comprehend that she was severely dependent on this kind of attention. In no time at all, she was in love again and simply continued into the relationship as though she had never suffered any heartbreak or pain before. It was only later when this relationship dissolved that she came to realize just how bad her relationship with herself was. She simply could not cope. Not mentioning her physical life and responsibilities, but emotionally she was so lost, and nothing that anybody told her to try and help would take effect at all. She became completely numb towards everyone and everything. She behaved almost as if someone had cut off all her limbs and dug her heart out. It was excruciatingly painful, and something Lisa said she never wants to experience ever again.

Chapter 5:

The Road to Recovery

Prevention certainly is better than curing. Although, every situation we find ourselves in is this simple, especially when it comes to matters of the psyche and our emotions. Recovering from any form of abuse is very challenging and is usually an extremely long and bumpy road. The good news is that there are ways to get better and avoid falling into the same cycle all over again.

The first thing we need to do is realize that we have survived already and that we need to acknowledge the fact that we are brave and so much stronger than we give ourselves credit for. There are steps we can take to start processing and dealing with our experience and be well on our way to recovery. Even though it takes time, it is important to be persistent, not give up our path, and ultimately, to find our true selves again.

First of all, learn to recognize manipulation when it occurs. It may not always be obvious or easy to spot, but trust your instincts. It is especially difficult when recognition involves someone you have a close relationship with, but keep in mind that it is because of the relationship that it is so easy for said person to use this tactic as it has worked so well in the past.

It is very possible that at this point in time we may not even know how to acknowledge our self-worth, let alone love ourselves the way we should. We feel lost, we do not know who we are anymore, and we question our own thoughts and feelings. It can be a good thing to take a time out and put some thought into the situation, whether it be about how we feel about what is said or how we are being treated. We need to ask ourselves if this is acceptable, not by social standards, but by our own intuition and judgement about what is happening.

As mentioned before, empaths are easy targets, and if you are indeed an empath, it may be necessary to rethink what is going on. Hopefully, by now, we have picked up on some habits of the abuser and can then learn to calculate very quickly if we are in fact being abused. We may find ourselves overwhelmed when we get even a small glimpse of our experience with an abuser. One of the hardest things to do is to come to terms with the abuse, and to try and not mentally or emotionally accuse an innocent person of abuse solely because they are expressing similar personality traits as our abuser.

Dealing with gaslighting and recovering from it may not always fall under the same umbrella, but it does go hand in hand for sure. Here are a few pointers to begin with:

- Call it out for what it is. If it walks like a duck and quacks like a duck, then it probably is a duck.

- You need to have patience and be gentle with your situation and with yourself.

- Try and surround yourself with as much love as possible. Reach out to friends and those you know to be loyal, who really love you, and only want the best for you.

- It cannot be stressed enough but learn from your past experiences. There should be no rush when it comes to healing.

- Remember that healing and moving forward is a lifelong process.

- Take responsibility for your own actions.

- It is very important to acknowledge yourself and how you feel more than you would have in the past.

- Acknowledge your feelings for what they are. If you are not sure about them, it is completely okay to dwell on them a bit in an attempt to figure things out for yourself.

- If you are in a position to get some help, then do so. There is absolutely no shame in asking for help. This is your life after all.

- Giving yourself time to heal is also very important. As mentioned before, there is absolutely no rush in the healing process; it is about you and you alone.

- It might be a good idea to form new relationships. At least not romantic ones, but do make new friends and become part of social circles again.

- Be honest with yourself. Are you doing the things you do to continuously please others, or are you now in it to win it?

- Learning to recognize gaslighting in the present will be a huge shift in your understanding of what it is and how to avoid it or the person who is potentially marking you as their victim.

- It might be a good idea to cultivate new hobbies, or perhaps revisit some of the things you used to love doing before everything turned around for the worst. As creatures of habit, we often forget to live in the moment and enjoy the little things. Reclaim those moments without apologizing for it

- Let the inner child live again. There is no reason for us to be too serious and forget to enjoy the little things. It is mostly those little things that keep our stress levels and anxiety in check in order for us to remain sane and continue with our daily lives

- If it is possible, reconnect with old friends, even if there was a long silence in the friendship. People are more understanding than we give them credit for and we should not be afraid to let them into our lives.

- If you are one of those people who have become quite judgmental on the onslaught, try and lessen this a little bit. Remember that we judge others the way we judge ourselves, and this might be a way of breaking out of that particular cycle as well.

- Read those self-help books. The more you learn and study, the better your chances of healing from all kinds of abuse you may have suffered.

- Listen to advice. Not everyone is out to get you, even though it feels this way sometimes. It is quite difficult to remember that not everyone you meet is abusive and step-by-step, teach yourself to learn to give a little trust. This is for your own good in the end.

- Apart from cultivating new hobbies, it could be useful to take up something, like yoga where you learn breathing exercises and things that can teach you how to stay calm and help you relax.

- The ever-overthinking mind needs a break too. Acknowledge your thoughts for what they are but do not entertain them too long. There is a difference between working through anger issues and just allowing negative thoughts to overcome you again. This is where those breathing techniques may come in handy.

The question most of us might have is: How does a narcissist get away with so much? They are experts in their field of manipulation, and they can simply be called chameleons by the way that they constantly change and adapt to their surroundings, situations, and the type of people they are dealing with. We also found that such people have the rude ability to smell out empaths as their targets.

Healing is difficult, not only because we need to work on ourselves, but we also have to come to terms with the things we have lost in the process and realize that some things we may never be able to regain. This, however, does in no way mean that we should never try, but we must learn to recognize when it is a futile exercise and should let go.

Letting go of an abuser is just as hard. Usually, we are the ones who truly do love the person who abuses us, and even though we know it is a lost cause, we will always hold on to the hope that things will get better if we give it more time and maybe work a little harder to make our partners happier. Perhaps if we change to suit them, things will become easier and they will love us once more the way they did before. Right here is where we need to decide if this person really loved us from the start or if we were just another toy in their collection because, in the end, that is exactly what we are, even if said relationship lasts a lifetime. We will then never really be certain of their past and how they treated other people unless we do some real homework and try and find as many facts and as much information as humanly possible to make any informed decisions in this regard. On the other hand, and sadly, many victims remain stuck in their situations because they feel too alone or too embarrassed to ask for help or to even mention any form of abuse to anybody outside of the relationship. Sometimes, the victim will simply accept the relationship as something normal and never really complain or confront the abuse. Other times, it is simply to keep the peace and continue feeding into the illusion that there is nothing wrong in the relationship, no matter how badly they are treated.

Setting Boundaries

On the path of healing yourself from past trauma or abuse, setting boundaries is probably one of the most important tasks we will need to conquer. The reason for this is because we will learn once again who we are as a person, recovering the identity we lost in the process of abuse. Terms such as "self-love" and "self-care" are actions we need to learn in order to move forward. We have to learn how to say no and not feel guilt over it. Re-establishing one's identity is no easy task, but we must learn once again to trust our instincts, and stop doing things to make others happy out of fear of being abandoned. Setting boundaries is a very important stepping stone and here are some useful tips:

- Start by saying no without harboring any guilt towards it and make a habit of saying no. The more you do it the easier it will get and in no time, you will have a solid foundation.

- Take another good look at your values. Are they what you desire from yourself and your life, or are they standing between you and your ultimate goals?

- The time has come for you to put your needs first, over and above everyone else. This is a very necessary step to take because you have forever taken care of other people's needs and forgotten your own. You have deprived yourself of so many great things. Please stop.

- Accept that you are not responsible for anyone else's actions or emotions. You cannot continuously sell yourself short for another person. Put yourself first at all times. Never forget you are no longer a victim and refuse to fall into old habits again.

- Whatever plans you make or goals you draw out for yourself, you need to see it through. It is very easy to make excuses as to why we are not getting things done, but it is also a sign that we do not deem ourselves important enough to achieve anything, no matter how small it is. Once you start with a project, for example, be sure to take it through to the end and finish it. This will also give you a great sense of accomplishment and fill you with satisfaction. If you can do this, you can do anything.

- Start believing in yourself more and in your abilities. Give yourself more credit. You deserve it.

Forgiving

The word forgiving is quite complex if we think about it. Some believe that forgiving someone who did us wrong is basically giving them an excuse to hurt us again, but for the most part, it has more to do with letting go of any anger or resentment that we may feel towards that person. We need to remember that living in anger towards another person hurts us more than the other person. We may feel that in order for us not to be taken advantage of again, not forgiving the other person might be the best way to prevent it. Although we cannot judge this decision made by someone else in their own situation and life path, we need to rethink this strategy.

Not only do we need to practice forgiveness towards others, but we also need to learn to forgive ourselves. We may not even actively realize it, but at some point, we do become our own worst enemies. We judge ourselves much more than we do others, and even more so than others would judge us. We judge others the way we judge ourselves, really. No matter how ridiculous this may sound, it is true in many ways. We can also go as far and say that what we see in others is what we see in ourselves. We are basically projecting our inner being onto others. This is not always a bad thing, but it can lead to conflict that could easily be avoided.

Part of the process of forgiving ourselves is realizing and accepting that what happened to us was not our fault. We did not ask for it. The abuser will certainly make a point of it to make us feel like we were fully deserving of what they dished out to us. We need to make a conscious decision every single day to stop blaming ourselves for any action taken by the abuser. Meaning we need to cease taking responsibility for the choices made by those who hurt us.

There are of course reasons we forgive people we care about because we do care about how they feel and we do not want to be the ones to hurt them. There are also steps we can take to practice forgiveness towards another person who hurt us:

- We may want to separate the person from their actions. Not all people are good or bad in such terms, we are all divided up into a bit of both. In reality, we will be good for the most part, but there are definitely people who will regard us as the bad guy in their story.

- Establish the intentions of the person and their actions. Even though someone has the tendency to be consciously hurtful towards us, not every situation may be part of their game. Everybody is allowed their own share of mistakes.

- It goes back to establishing boundaries between yourself and others.

- Forgiving can create stronger bonds between people, especially if the person hurting you is not someone you can easily walk away from. Showing a bit of humanity to another person, even if it is one who is abusing you, may open them up a little more and hopefully, they will also start to realize how their actions have been affecting you. After all, we do want the best for those we care about, and we should strive to be the type of person who is willing to help another instead of being too judgmental. Keep in mind that this does not mean that we are giving the abuser more ammunition to use against us

- It is important to stand your ground. Communication is key and this will probably take some time to learn, but it is a good tool to use when you need to protect yourself from any fighter abuse.

- An important aspect of forgiving is to not forget so easily. It is also a form of self-respect and connects to the previous point

- Once you have decided to forgive, refrain from bringing up the past all the time. This is a tactic an abuser will use to weaken you emotionally and is effective in making you doubt yourself. It is harmful and also means that you have trouble letting go of something you thought you closed the book on. In a case like this, take the opportunity to deal with it at that point than keep hanging on to it and deal with it at a later stage, if it keeps coming up, then it is clearly still an issue, and it is not healthy for you either.

- Forgiving also demonstrates that you need to be treated better and that there is always room for improvement, whatever the situation is at the time.

- Forgiveness is a sign of self-improvement and growth, just as setting boundaries are a sign of growing stronger and more mature.

- If nothing else, forgiving is a fantastic tool to keep anger in check. Anger in itself is quite harmful, and more so towards ourselves than another person. Having to live with unresolved anger issues over time becomes like a ticking time bomb. It can be very dangerous for yourself and those around you.

- It is also an indication that we accept and understand that we cannot change other people. Only they can do what they feel is necessary.

On our life path of healing and finding ourselves again, we sometimes forget that the only things we can change or have the power to change are ourselves. This truth is instrumental to the fact that we need to take care of ourselves and be the best we can be.

On the road to recovery, leave no stone unturned. During this time, it is good to question everything because this is a journey where we are seeking the truth and an escape out of a very dark hole. We often must face this journey alone so it can become quite a lonely road. The belief is that if we stick to our goals, we will start finding answers and our escape route. Hopefully, we then can come out stronger on the other end, which is the best any of us survivors can hope for, and on our journey. We also hope to have encouraged others in our position to take the lead in their own lives and become stronger to escape the clutches of abuse, never to fall into the trap again.

Conclusion

With all this information at hand, the story of abuse, being a victim, survival, and the road to recovery becomes clearer and prevents the risk of any one of us falling prey to an abusive predator. But don't get too comfortable because no one is safe. Not safe from manipulation, gaslighting, or narcissism, which all go hand-in-hand in most emotional and mental abuse cases. We have seen just how damaging it can be and the depths of darkness we can so easily fall into.

Not only is it absolutely heartbreaking, but it is of utmost importance to become aware of such abuses, and it is our responsibility to stop looking the other way and continuously give the other person the upper hand and the power to control us. We need to take back our humanity, humility, self-respect, and refuse to become a puppet in another person's plight for power.

So far, we have come to understand that we have no control over other people and their thoughts, feelings, or actions, and at the same time, we need to realize that we too are just as responsible for our own actions as much as we expect the next person to be for their own. We all want to be better people in general and as a whole, but some people around us make it very difficult for us by throwing curveballs around every corner. We need to be prepared for just about anything, and the best way to go about it is to educate ourselves and study people and their personalities.

Think about it like this: If we do not come to understand the different aspects of human nature, we may never understand what abuse is, why some people seem to practice it so easily and without remorse, and we may never be able to break free and heal from it.

We have also come to know that unresolved abuses that stem from childhood will certainly be carried into adulthood, and thus, we may become the abusers we are trying to get away from. For some victims, it is okay to want to understand why their abusers do what they do. All abuse starts from somewhere; and if we can understand the elements which caused the abuse, we can also find different ways in which to deal with such people and at the same time help ourselves.

Although sexual abuse is not discussed here, it is also a good example to use if we want to express just how severe gaslighting and narcissistic abuse is, just to connect the dots between the fine lines of being abused to becoming an abuser. It is perhaps one of the easiest ways to explain the cycle of abuse because physical abuse is much more obvious than abuse of the psyche.

Insecurity, worthlessness, hopelessness, and fear are among the most common symptoms of severe abuse. These are also some of the hardest issues to overcome, but even harder to begin to deal with because we would have to go through it all again, mentally and emotionally, to come to terms with it and begin the path of acceptance that we still cannot change other people. It is imperative to know that we as victims cannot blame ourselves for any of an abuser's actions. Our abusers will certainly go out of their way to make us feel as if we are completely at fault and it always works. It really is only part of a vicious cycle of back-and-forth manipulation until we doubt ourselves to the point that we cannot tell the difference between our realities and truths anymore.

As we have seen, it is not easy having to deal with abusers but it is of the utmost importance to do so to ensure our survival in what is already such a cruel world. This the same world we are trying to protect our children from, and hopefully, successfully teach them how to not fall into the same habits or traps we too were not taught to avoid. In all honesty, this may be the only silver lining out of all the negativity that was forced upon us as victims, but it is also a great tool to use for any future relationships that we might have, especially the ones with ourselves.

Within all of this, we must have learned that if we put our own needs first from time to time and pay more attention to our own feelings. Instead of feeding our little bits of happiness to others, we may just have a better chance of getting out of abusive relationships quicker and heal faster, or at least be on the road to recovery much sooner.

The cycle of abuse needs to be broken, this cannot be stressed enough, and the first step is to start setting boundaries. We need to demonstrate that we are serious in our establishment and that we will not allow people to walk all over us. Yet, we are all guilty of this, we are extremely tolerant as human beings, and it is indeed one of the features that make us so incredibly unique and special. However, it is this very fact that also allows people with their hidden, ugly agendas to take advantage of us and see how far they can push us before we reach a breaking point, and in some cases, how far they can actually break us.

In the end, it will always be up to us to decide how much abuse we are willing to take and what part we play in abusive relationships, if we are in real danger, and how to deal with such dangers should we come face to face with it. Nobody but us can take responsibility for ourselves, draw a clear line, and make the necessary changes to lead us into better and happier lives.

References

8 Ways to Deal with Gaslighting. (2020, June 25). Healthline. https://www.healthline.com/health/how-to-deal-with-gaslighting

20 Heartbreaking Signs of a Manipulative Mother. (2020, February 21). Toxic Ties. https://toxicties.com/manipulative-mother-signs/

Center, N. R. (2018, October 17). *13 Warning Signs of Codependency | How to Treat Codependency.* Nova Recovery Center near Austin Texas. https://novarecoverycenter.com/addiction/13-warning-signs-codependency/

Coburn, J. (2019, April 4). *How to Heal After the Emotional Abuse of Gaslighting.* The Mighty. https://themighty.com/2019/04/how-to-recover-from-gaslighting-emotional-abuse/

Eckelkamp, S. (2018, September 12). *9 Signs You're in a Relationship With a Total Narcissist.* Prevention. https://www.prevention.com/health/mental-health/g19876574/narcissistic-personality-disorder-symptoms/#:~:text=%20But%20there%20is%20a%20tipping%20point%20you

Hakki, M. (2019, September 3). *8 unmistakable signs you are a victim of gaslighting.* I Heart Intelligence.com. https://iheartintelligence.com/signs-you-are-victim-of-gaslighting/

Hartney, E. (2008, November 14). *The Cycle of Sexual Abuse and Abusive Adult Relationships.* Verywell Mind; Verywellmind. https://www.verywellmind.com/the-cycle-of-sexual-abuse-22460

How to Deal with Gaslighting in 6 Easy Steps | Marriage.com. (2019, June 6). Marriage Advice - Expert Marriage Tips & Advice. https://www.marriage.com/advice/mental-health/how-to-deal-with-gaslighting/

How to Deal With Guilt-Tripping From a Manipulative Parent. (2021, January 31). Toxic Ties. https://toxicties.com/manipulative-parent-guilt-tripping/#:~:text=%20Here%20is%20a%203-step%20approach%20to%20dealing

How to Recover from Gaslighting. (n.d.). WikiHow. Retrieved March 30, 2022, from https://www.wikihow.com/Recover-from-Gaslighting#:~:text=Because%20it%20is%20a%20form%20of%20abuse%2C%20gaslighting

https://www.facebook.com/selfcarehaven. (2019, April 4). *20 Diversion Tactics Highly Manipulative Narcissists, Sociopaths And Psychopaths Use To Silence You.* Thought Catalog; Thought Catalog. https://thoughtcatalog.com/shahida-arabi/2016/06/20-diversion-tactics-highly-manipulative-narcissists-sociopaths-and-psychopaths-use-to-silence-you/

Kokoski, C. (2021, February 19). *35 Types of Gaslighting Manipulators Use Against You.* Heart Affairs. https://medium.com/heart-affairs/35-types-of-gaslighting-manipulators-use-against-you-3b3f0481d7af

Lamb, S. (2020, January 21). *What Do Gaslighting, Codependency, and Narcissism Have in Common?* The Good Men Project. https://goodmenproject.com/featured-content/what-do-gaslighting-codependency-and-narcissism-have-in-common/

LMHC, R. A. S., & MS. (2021, June 11). *The Dysfunctional Family and Codependency.* Aion Recovery. https://aionrecovery.com/articles/the-dysfunctional-family-and-codependency/

Luna, A. (2015, March 6). *You're Not Going Crazy: 15 Signs You're a Victim of Gaslighting.* LonerWolf. https://lonerwolf.com/gaslighting/#:~:text=

When%20it%20comes%20to%20gaslighting%2 C%20empaths%20are%20easy

Manipulation (psychology). (2021, October 17). Wikipedia. https://en.wikipedia.org/wiki/Manipulation_(p sychology)

Manson, M. (2014, January 9). *How We Judge Others is How We Judge Ourselves*. Mark Manson. https://markmanson.net/how-we-judge-others

Milnes, A. (2019, February 14). *15 Signs You Are In a Relationship With a Narcissist (And What to Do)*. Lifehack. https://www.lifehack.org/823381/relationship-with-a-narcissist

Olivier, M. (2017, October 3). *5 Ways To Start Setting Boundaries After Emotional Abuse - Melany Oliver's Blog*. Melany Oliver. https://melany-oliver.com/5-ways-to-start-setting-boundaries-after-emotional-abuse/

Pace, R. (2022, January 12). *20 Reasons to Forgive but Not Forget in Relationships*. Marriage Advice - Expert Marriage Tips & Advice. https://www.marriage.com/advice/forgiveness /reasons-to-forgive-but-not-forget/

Problems of Codependents. (2016, May 17). Psych Central. https://psychcentral.com/lib/problems-of-codependents#4

Selva, J. (2018, February 9). *Codependency: What Are The Signs & How To Overcome It.* PositivePsychology.com. https://positivepsychology.com/codependency-definition-signs-worksheets/#:~:text=Codependency%20refers%20to%20a%20psychological

Spencer, E. (2021, November 16). *20 Signs of a Narcissistic Relationship That'll Destroy You Slowly.* LovePanky - Your Guide to Better Love and Relationships. https://www.lovepanky.com/my-life/relationships/16-clear-signs-youre-in-a-narcissistic-relationship#:~:text=A%20common%20symptom%20of%20being%20in%20a%20narcissistic

The Role Codependency in Abusive Relationships. (2020, May 13). Narcissist Abuse Support. https://narcissistabusesupport.com/the-role-codependency-in-abusive-relationships/

Valecha, K. (2020, August 15). *12 Warning Signs Of Gaslighting And 5 Ways To Deal With It.* Bonobology.com. https://www.bonobology.com/warning-signs-of-gaslighting-ways-to-deal-with-it/#:~:text=1.%20Denial%20%E2%80%93%20the%20most%20common%20sign%20of

Villines, Z. (2018, August 7). *Codependency and Narcissism May Have More in Common Than You Think.* GoodTherapy.org Therapy Blog. https://www.goodtherapy.org/blog/codependency-narcissism-may-have-more-in-common-than-you-think-0807187#:~:text=Core%20symptoms%20of%20codependency%20are%20shared%3A%20Denial%2C%20Shame

What is the difference between love and pity? (n.d.). Quora. Retrieved April 4, 2022, from https://www.quora.com/What-is-the-difference-between-love-and-pity

Why healing is important after an abusive relationship. (2021, April 18). Www.nafisahnk.com. https://www.nafisahnk.com/blog/healing-abuse-relationship

Wikipedia Contributors. (2019a, January 13). *Charles Manson.* Wikipedia; Wikimedia Foundation. https://en.wikipedia.org/wiki/Charles_Manson

Wikipedia Contributors. (2019b, January 27). *Jim Jones.* Wikipedia; Wikimedia Foundation. https://en.wikipedia.org/wiki/Jim_Jones